The Grounding Book

by Josh Schultz

www.thrivemeditation.com

This book is dedicated to my sister, Sara Wolf. You are a very capable spirit who I love so much and I am honored to work with you in this lifetime Sara.

Thank you Nicole Wright for repeatedly reminding and encouraging me to take action to make this book happen; it wouldn't have happened without your loving support. And thank you Judith Catalano for kicking so much ass; you made my program the experience of a lifetime. Chihiro and Vandana – thanks for supporting me all the way through. Katherine Morrill, thank you for all your help and consistent dedication – working with you has been so much fun.

And much gratitude to Rick, Lisa, and Trish for stepping out of the box to create something truly novel. Also, thank you Melanie, Linda, Kathy, Isah, Jason, Pasha, and Eula for all your insights. Lastly, I appreciate everything you taught me Tony Thompson, Allan Prentice, Mary Raftery, Paula Dennis, Heather Lauren, Richard Pozzuto, Carmen Figueras, Marc Shargel, Brooke Scudder, Jon Cooke, & Benedicte Last. You are all amazing teachers.

Table of Contents

Introduction

MY PERSONAL STORY

I spent two years studying with professional psychics in a clairvoyant training program; I learned from top San Francisco Bay Area clairvoyants and I am privileged to be able to call them my friends and have them as part of my social and professional networks. The information in this book is unique indeed. Many of the ideas and tips in this book you cannot currently find elsewhere. Some of them I created myself. Please consider that you have probably saved yourself at least several months, or years, of energy work by getting the information in this book.

I wrote this book because of how important grounding is and how long it took myself and other people I knew to fully realize its importance. I spent many years out of body experiencing all kinds of amazing things, yet everyone I talked to said that I needed to "get grounded."

But being out of body was fun; I could experience all kinds of weird and wild stuff anytime I wanted. I could feel the deep bond between two birds by moving my awareness into their space; my entire body would vibrate and I could hear music when I meditated on being inside distant stars. Life was a kind of perpetual psychedelic trip; and being in the body was painful because there was so much foreign energy and core issues I was reluctant to look at and deal with. Many people go out of body (i.e., disassociate), and stay out, as a way to feel safe. When you have a grounding cord it is much easier to be in your body.

Grounding is, fundamentally, a way to release everyone else from your space – their judgments, limitations, expectations, energy, emotions, pictures, etc. And when you do that, you can begin to create more space for yourself. You can create what you want and have it come to you in the way that you want. When everyone else's energy is in your body you end up unconsciously creating for other people. So by grounding, you begin to own your personal power and energetic space. Most people are completely unaware that someone else's energy could be in their space and do not know how to differentiate it from their own energy or emotions. Grounding is a way to start to release what isn't yours and begin to understand that level of differentiation in your consciousness.

Chapter 1 – The Basics

WHAT WILL THIS BOOK COVER?

This book will cover what grounding is, what it is not, and minor, yet imperative, details about grounding, which can have a tremendous impact on your relationships, spiritual growth, and general enjoyment of your body and life. If you are empathic, or feel like you are taking on all kinds of emotions or energy that isn't yours, then learning how to be in your body and ground will help you tremendously! Grounding is the foundation upon which energy work lies.

WHY GROUND?

Foreign energy in your body often creates pain. Grounding releases it. Foreign energy in your body can act as a block or invalidation in your space. Grounding releases everyone else's emotions and energy from your body and helps release your own stuck emotions. Releasing foreign energy feels absolutely wonderful. Grounding will allow you to enjoy your body more and will allow you to create more of what *you* want in your life. Grounding has even has gained popularity in PTSD therapy due to its effectiveness at reducing stress.

Knowing how to replenish your own energy with golden energy is a vital tool to have as well – or grounding excessively can exhaust you to the point of insatiable hunger or exhaustion.

HOW DO YOU GROUND?

Grounding is a very simple tool – you imagine a connection, or cord, extending from your 1st chakra/tailbone into the center of the planet. It can be very simple, yet very powerful.

Note: *Do not use black, white, or silver for your grounding cord (more on that later).*

Sit upright and relax your body. Feel yourself in your body. Rub your feet on the ground. Imagine your feet chakras opening up like the lens of a camera. Or maybe you see a door opening or a light getting bigger. Use an image that works for you. See it with as much detail as possible; if you can't see it then just pretend – your subconscious mind is powerful enough to know what to do. So allow your feet chakras to open up. Next, touch your tailbone and locate your root chakra. Just recognize it; it can be very easy to just notice what you notice there. Now imagine a cord coming out of your root chakra and imagine that it extends all the way down to the center of the planet; this is your grounding cord. It could be a rainbow, or a waterfall, a rope, or a series of columns. Your grounding cord can be anything you choose. It could even be a stack of flowers, or a bunch of monkeys. What color is your grounding cord? Imagine it with as much detail as you would like.

Next imagine how your grounding cord connects into your root chakra and how it connects to the center of the earth. Does it use a hook or a tie to connect to your first chakra? Maybe you imagine an anchor connecting it to the center of the earth or imagine your cord has roots like a tree. Or maybe something else completely – there is no right or wrong choice. You can use anything that comes to mind. Notice and enjoy how securely your grounding cord is connected to you. And notice how securely you are connected to the earth.

Your grounding cord allows all foreign energy in your body to release with ease. Imagine yourself pulling in your aura in nice and tight around your body and imagine that you are tucking it into your grounding cord around your first chakra. This allows you to release all the miscellaneous energy floating around in your space.

Allow yourself to just sit for 10-20 minutes grounding like this – noticing how it feels to release energy, thoughts, worries, emotions, and concerns down that grounding cord. Next, bring some earth energy into your body by imagining two cords coming out of your feet chakras and going deep into the earth. When you use your grounding cord you connect to the center of the earth, but when you bring in earth energy imagine it coming from deep within the earth – but not the center of it. Imagine that earth energy is effortlessly rising up into your feet chakras. You can experiment with pushing energy out through your feet chakras as well if you like.

Think of 10 different cords and try using them all. Blow up the old one and create a new one. How does each one feel? Ground in different situations and notice how you feel different. This will really help you master knowing how grounding affects you.

You can ground lying down, but our energy tends to move upward, and out of body, when we lie down because that is what happens when we sleep. A big misconception is that you have to be able to visualize really well in order to ground. This is completely untrue; if you can't visualize at all you can still ground extremely effectively. Your sub-conscious mind will handle it, just tell it what to do and imagine that it is happening.

OPEN YOUR FEET CHAKRAS AS MUCH AS YOU CAN

I highly recommend purchasing Robert Bruce's book titled *Energy Work* and practicing his exercises to open up your feet chakras; this will help your ability to ground tremendously. Even if all you can do is 10-30 minutes a day you will be able to make good progress opening up your feet chakras. Many meditators spend months, and years, working on their feet chakras. You can use the image of a golden hammer and chisel directly on the feet chakras as a way to tap out foreign energy. Or you can create a colorful golf ball sized sphere about an inch below each foot; slice each ball diagonally – one in one direction and the other in the opposite; pull the halves apart slightly and start rotating them in opposite directions. That is a good technique for stimulating your feet chakras and moving out energy. Additionally, you might imagine someone lightly grazing the insides of your feet chakras with a twisting quill or soft brush. Or try using the energy of a stream flowing through them; play around with different visualizations and environments.

You can also massage your feet regularly, which helps. Additionally, you can get a tennis ball or a golf ball and roll your foot around on it. Being able to open them up by moving your awareness, like with Robert Bruce's exercises, is best though. Doing micro-movements with your toes will also help push energy out when you get bored. When you work to open them up initially you may start to have splitting pains or sensations in your nose and that is normal. One sign you are making decent progress is if your sense of smell increases significantly to the point where you can smell energy. The centermost foot chakras look somewhat like an opaque basketball net, which surrounds a network of energetic channels inside it. You essentially want to widen the opening of this chakra as far as possible and then pull out the energy from the channels, and repeat ad infinitum. Of course you can work the heel chakras, and the toe chakras as well. Grounding through the feet can be extremely tedious and time consuming, but it works and is highly effective.

Chapter 2 – What Grounding Isn't

One problem is that people use the singular terminology "to ground" to mean several different things – hence the reason confusion arises so easily over this concept. This is also probably the reason people fail to recognize the necessity and magnitude of grounding.

There is a big difference between being in your body, shifting your focus (or awareness) around/inside your body, validating your body, having lots of earth energy in your body, and the act of "grounding" out, or releasing, energy from your body into the earth.

BEING IN YOUR BODY

Being in your body is basically just having your aura pulled in nice and tight around your body – usually around 1 to 3 feet. Some people refer to being "grounded" when what they really mean is "being in your body as a spirit." When your aura is pulled in you will be able to feel and experience your body much more.

Experiment with how it feels to have your aura expanded at different lengths.

If you can, have someone sit down and experiment with feeling their aura, with your opened hand chakras. Have them pull it in real tight and feel it with your hand chakras; then have them expand it out further and feel the difference.

BEING OUT OF YOUR BODY

Having your awareness out of your body is equivalent to having your aura expanded further than approximately 6 feet. Again this number is not set in stone. Your experience of having your aura expanded is going to be different from mine. However, when my awareness is out of my body I feel like I am "floating," "spacy," or "spaced-out." Qualities I personally experience being out of my body include: feeling invisible around others, being unaffected by cold temperatures, and the sense that objects in the room are moving when I move, as if I am tipsy or drunk.

One example of how you might tell that your aura is perpetually expanded is if electrical objects and lights frequently go out when you are around. The original mental process that allowed me to move my awareness out of my body was thinking, "I don't want to be here." If you are constantly doing things you don't want to be doing, and going places you really don't want to be going, then this may be causing you to be out of your body, but there are also many other reasons as well.

SHIFTING YOUR AWARENESS

Shifting your awareness is just focusing on something. It is possible to have your point of awareness (or "assemblage point") in any imaginable place inside, or outside, your body. When you move your point of awareness, your state of mind changes and, consequently, how you feel changes. You can move your point of awareness out of your body and into other people, trees, stars, animals, objects, etc. You can shift your awareness way down into your tailbone or stomach and feel strong and grounded; however, it is important not to confuse this with grounding. Some meditation techniques may advise "grounding" yourself by consciously focusing on your root chakra, but this is more of a shifting technique. Just focusing on your root chakra will not necessarily release energy from your space, although it may be helpful in bringing energy to your awareness; there is a big difference between stationary focusing and grounding. Generally, you want to keep your point of awareness in the *center of your head* most of the time, especially if you want to develop your clairvoyance. Of course there is nothing wrong with moving your awareness down into your feet or first chakra and it can feel absolutely amazing to do so.

VALIDATING YOUR BODY

Many people talk about being grounded when they are actually referring to, "validating your body." For example: eating a healthy diet, eating meat, sleeping, exercising, yoga, bathing in sea salts, hiking, massage, sex, beer, chocolate, rock'n'roll, etc. It is definitely important to validate your body. Deep tissue massage work is extremely beneficial in becoming grounded; when you open up your pelvic floor and get your body in alignment you will be able to ground with more ease. Being in nature regularly is also absolutely imperative. The forest, and the ocean, strip away huge amounts of foreign energy from your space.

Sometimes you will have to pull up as much earth energy as you possibly can in order to balance out all of the releasing that is happening. Movement practices also fall into this category. Learn how to move your body in a way that validates it; so whether you are on the yoga mat or making a sandwich, you are moving in a way that validates your body.

HAVING EARTH ENERGY IN YOUR BODY

Earth energy is energy from the earth. Go ahead and imagine your feet chakras opening and cords connecting from your feet down into the earth. Practice pulling earth energy up into your *space through these cords connected to your feet*. Allow it to come into your feet and run up your legs and into your pelvis. You can run that energy back down your main grounding cord or let it come into your whole body. How does it feel? What color is it? Again, avoid black, white, and silver. If you're not sure what color you're bringing in you can always choose a color. Sometimes people refer to others as "being grounded" or "down to earth" when what they often mean is someone who runs a lot of earth energy through their space – or someone who is stuck operating from the first chakra. You can also practice running earth energy through different places in your body and notice how you feel and what happens to your space.

You can run earth energy from Hawaii through your body even if you are sitting in New York. Experiment with running earth energy from different places through your feet, legs, and down your grounding cord. What if you reverse the flow of earth energy? How does that feel?

Chapter 3 – What can you Ground?

Anything. You can literally give anything a ground cord. You can ground pets, family members, friends, strangers, cars, airplanes, computers, books, entire rooms, parking spots, movie seats, your shoulder, your knee, any pain, your solar plexus, your testicles/ovaries, your head.

So your grounding cord does not always have to be from your tailbone to the center of the earth; it can be from the center of your head to the earth, etc. Ground the center of your head regularly. Always ground other people, and animals, with their own energy. When you give them a grounding cord just imagine that it comes down from their own energy. If you use your own energy to ground the person then you will create karma with them, which you don't want.

My massage therapist grounds himself, his clients, whatever body part he is working on, as well as the room he is working in. If you are a massage therapist it will be helpful to also visualize your aura being "pulled in" tight or close to your body so that you are not in your client's space.

Back when I was habitually out of body my third chakra was always on over-drive; so when I started to get over excited or nervous it really helped to ground my third chakra or wherever else anxiety arose from in my space. When I feel pain I ground it and it drains away. At fancy restaurants I want the best seat in the house; so I ground it a few days before the meal. Ground good parking spots for yourself before you even leave your house.

Ground your genetics. Ground sub-personalities like your judgment or your frustration or your analyzer. Ground trying, and effort. Ground agreements, habits, and patterns you have with family or friends, which may be blocking you. Ground your route before you drive somewhere: see a rose where you are now; ground it, connect it to the Divine Source. Then see a rose at your destination and ground that rose and connect it to the Divine Source. Then connect the two roses with a golden line. Ground lost objects to help find them. And most importantly, ground yourself! *This list consists of weeks of things to play with in your meditation space. Apply each of them.*

Chapter 4 – The Secrets

KEEPING YOUR GROUNDING CORD IN PRESENT TIME

This tiny tid-bit of information is hugely important. This means that you need to use different grounding cords often. Use a different grounding cord every time you move into a significantly different situation. The reason for this is that you want to always keep your grounding cord in present time. If you use the same grounding cord all the time, what happens is that it tends to get frayed, clogged, or otherwise stuck. Blow up, or destroy, your old cord and create a new one. Another way I like to bring my grounding cord into the present is to imagine it vibrating at the brightest gold I possibly can and then take a look at, and tell myself, the current date and time.

EXPERIMENT WITH DIFFERENT GROUNDING CORDS

What does it feel like to use a green garden hose for your grounding cord? What about a waterfall? Come up with new cords every day. Use a rainbow, tree roots, cobalt blue glass, monkeys; the list of possibilities is endless. You could try a lay of Hawaiian flowers, as pictured in this book. Definitely use different colors. Using different grounding cords helps you to keep your grounding in present time. Also different grounding cords have different properties. So a waterfall might make you feel significantly different from tree roots. It is good to know when each one works best for you and how they each feel. It also makes your meditation space fun, rather than boring and repetitive. And it is a lot easier to release energy when you are having fun, rather than when you are in a serious state of mind; seriousness vibrates very closely to control energy and will just make things significantly harder for yourself.

SIZE MATTERS FOR GROUNDING CORDS

The width of your grounding cord matters too. Sometimes people make them as large as an entire room or building. This will allow you to release more energy. Also, be sure that your grounding cord is balanced on both sides of your body. Your grounding cord can be as big as you want! Usually the size of your hips works well.

CREATE AND DESTROY; CREATE AND DESTROY...

If you're grounding connection isn't working then sometimes you may have to go through 10 cords one after another – destroying the old one, creating a new one, destroying that one and creating another new one...and on and on until your sub-conscious mind "gets it." This usually becomes necessary when you have a lot of stuck energy in your space.

AVOIDING WHITE, BLACK, AND SILVER.

White is usually a high vibrational transmedium energy. You don't want that in your grounding because then beings can easily get in there and mess with your ability to ground. Black is usually heavy energy and hides things easily so you don't want to use that either. Silver is usually foreign energy that is "not from this world." If you are seeing white or silver in your grounding and then soon after, or during, your meditation you get a sudden urge to take a nap, fall asleep, or go unconscious, then you want to definitely get rid of, and separate yourself from, those energies.

GOLDEN REVITALIZATION

Golden revitalization is how you replenish your energy! After grounding you create empty space in your aura. Do not leave it empty or someone else's energy will fill it up. Replenish yourself with your highest creative essence often! It is very simple to do. Just imagine a gigantic sphere of *golden energy* above your head and tell yourself (i.e., postulate) that it is only your highest creative energy. Rub your hands together to help stimulate and open up your hand chakras and then bring down the golden sphere you created above your head into your entire body. What you are really doing with this visualization is bringing in your own spirit's higher energy from the eighth chakra.

You have to fill in your aura/space with your own energy or guess what happens? Someone else will come along and just dump their energy into the space you just cleared up! Feel what it is like to just bring in gold energy all day long. This will really give you a good idea of how it affects you. Golden revitalization will also tend to make you more aware of foreign energy in your space too.

Size Matters for Golden Revitalization

This took me a while to discover and was only mentioned to me casually by a teacher of mine. Please realize that this single tip alone is worth the price of this book if you are serious about grounding. When I was first grounding I was doing it for upwards of 6 hours a day and completely exhausted myself because I did not know about this one tiny piece of information.

Most people *grossly underestimate* the amount of energy they release when they ground. If you're grounding a lot and bringing in a golden sphere the size of a basketball then you aren't replenishing your energy enough. It is ok to bring in huge golden spheres, the size of an entire valley, or the size of a star! This is a very minor detail, but may mean the difference between feeling completely exhausted or replenished! It helps quite a bit to really imagine how big it is above your head and how it looks. And for some people it's not the size that matters, but the number of times they replenish themselves with gold energy.

Chapter 5 – Advanced Grounding Topics

Although grounding is very simple it becomes more complicated when you start using it regularly and recognize all the conditions and interrelated elements of yourself as well as your energy system and environment. All of these things effect how well you can ground.

There is all the third chakra energy in your body which has conditioned how, and how much, you are able to actually "be in your body" to ground in the first place. Then there is all the foreign control energy in your body that doesn't want you to be in your body. Then there are all the people corded into you who are actually running their energy through you for all kinds of different reasons. Of course you can ground all this stuff out, but many people doing meditation won't recognize any of this. Please realize that those three categories of energy are a tremendous project for most people to work on – taking months and often years to work through. *Look at them in your own meditation space.*

Other people may be energetically corded, i.e., connected, into you and draining your energy or dumping their energy into you; it is important to remove these cords. People are able to cord into you through pictures in your space that you have not destroyed or become neutral to. Often grounding will release other people's cords from your space; and sometimes the person that you severed the connection to will immediately try to contact you to re-establish a connection.

However, grounding may not always work to get rid of certain cords, because in order for a cord to form you have to create some kind of conscious or unconscious agreement with another being. And if you don't end your agreements with others then it is possible that they will just end up grounding through you – essentially using you as a virtual energy dumpster. It is also possible for people/cords to be a drain on your energy – leaving you feeling weak and empty – so grounding actually ends up exacerbating the problem. And if you don't know how to replenish yourself energetically then grounding excessively can become a dangerous situation.

If you are the most grounded person in the room or even in your neighborhood then others will sometimes see that unconsciously and start to *ground through you*! So it is good to sometimes hold a mental picture, or imaginary flashcard, out in front of you to that person and show them that they can ground themselves.

Then there is ambient energy and household agreements. If the ambient energy around you is nasty then when you ground you will just end up bringing all that junk into your body. You have to be able to ground and energetically hold the environmental space around you. If you have controlling family members, picky/intrusive landlords, or troublesome roommates then this can be tricky or just a downright waste of your time to meditate in that environment. Some people do not want you to ground or do energy meditation in a shared space and they will actually try to block you from doing so. In short, you need your own physical space that you can make your own sanctuary.

HOW TO GROUND AND OWN A ROOM

Simply imagine a grounding cord the size of the room going from the floor to the center of the earth. That will ground the room. You can also imagine bringing in some neutral golden cosmic energy and flush out the ambient energy down the grounding cord with that gold. Now there is also another subject called *owning* a space. This is where *you consciously set the energy* of a room, or space, at a color or vibration or picture that you want. You can do this by imagining golden columns at every corner of the room or golden balls at every corner. Let those golden columns, or balls, connect to another golden column, or ball, in the center of the room and ground them all down to the center of the earth. That allows you to own the room. Then you can either mentally draw your name on each wall or paste a picture of a rose or other object on each wall; that energetically defines the perimeter of the space.

Do not own other people's spaces, especially professional ones like the dentist's office, or the doctor's office, or an opera. In order for them to do their job comfortably *they have to own* the space for themselves. They are, of course, most likely doing it all on an unconscious level, but you don't want to go in there and mess up their routine; if you change the energy they may not be able to operate as they usually do and you don't want your dentist to make a mistake. You can however ground any physical location, professional or otherwise, and it will be okay. Grounding a space is different from owning, and setting the energy for, a space.

You can own the energy of public places, like restaurants. A lot of times, in my past, I liked things more quiet, and with less bustle, so I would set the energy of the restaurants and bars I ate at to a vibration of emptiness. What usually happened is that most people would unconsciously start to match that energy on their seventh chakras and go along with it; and soon enough I would be the only person sitting at that bar or table in the whole place.

It is possible to ground any part of your body or energy system. You can ground through your feet, but this is usually very time consuming and requires significant commitment. It works and I've spent countless hours doing it. And like I said before, you can ground your head, heart, hands, kidneys, ovaries, testes, knees, etc too. A good meditation is to play around with grounding different parts of your body and notice what energy comes out and what pictures/images come to mind.

GIVE YOUR GROUNDING AN UPDATE

You want to regularly update your grounding capability and capacity. As you do it more this will automatically happen, but it is a great idea to start consciously doing it and owning how you want to ground and use the ability for yourself.

Your grounding cord can also be effected by crisis and other kinds of experiences. Imagine how your ability to ground might change if you came face to face with a mountain lion; you might go into survival mode and start running a lot of fear energy. So ideally, you want to create a grounding cord that is strong and capable enough to handle that situation.

Try meditating and grounding when your friends or significant other is doing something very distracting. You may have noticed your grounding getting cut off. That is a great opportunity to update your grounding cord/information to be able to withstand physical distraction. However, it may take some initial practice with the tool before you are able to update your information so quickly, because you need to have a degree of unconscious competence, i.e., skill, first.

SUPREME BEING UPDATES

Next time you are in meditation have the Supreme Being (God) give your grounding cord a "update" or a "special coating." This really seems to be powerful and fun! You don't have to know every last detail of how to do it; you can just postulate that it is happening and let yourself have it. I like to see a gold column of light connecting my grounding to the Divine Source when I do this exercise; imagine your grounding cord vibrating at the highest gold color you can see. *Try this in your next meditation space.*

OTHER UPDATES

All of these updates are designed to be done *in a meditation space*. Update your own grounding cord by meditating on how your grounding would be if you had been doing it for 25 more years. Add all that capability, experience, and potential into your current grounding cord, just with your imagination. *Notice the difference.*

Ground and meditate on how thinking about different kinds of crisis experiences change your grounding cord. When you imagine losing your job and all your money how does your grounding change? What do you feel? Update your current grounding cord (and information) and just imagine creating a new grounding cord that is capable and strong enough to withstand that possible experience. Try the same thing with an earthquake, or maybe someone who is hysterical on the other end of the phone. Update your grounding cord to be able to handle all of these things with ease.

You also don't want to condition your ability to ground to

be dependent upon where you habitually do grounding meditation. Practice everywhere and anywhere and under different conditions. This is called the SAID principle – Specific Adaption to Imposed Demand. Your body adapts to exactly what you do, how you do it. So don't condition yourself in ways that end up becoming limitations. Ground while hiking, walking, driving, working, talking on the phone, etc.

The picture you choose for your grounding cord/connection also has a strong influence on how effective your ability to ground is. The qualities of the picture you choose actually effect your energy. So if you choose redwood tree roots then don't be surprised if you see foreign energy trying to claw its way back up your cord when you ground. Something like a slippery tube might be more effective, or it might not. It's all in your imagination – and your imagination is very powerful and real on an energy level and to your sub-conscious mind.

GROUNDING THROUGH FAMILY PICTURES

One thing you want to look at clairvoyantly, i.e., in meditation, is your mother and father's information on grounding. How do they ground? You want to make sure that you are grounding through *your pictures and information.* For example, if your father grounds through violence and your mother grounds through hoarding (illogical I know), but you ground through playing then you will want to energetically separate from their pictures by becoming aware of where those pictures are in your space and then blowing them up outside your aura. Otherwise, you may find yourself collecting things unnecessarily and channeling psychotic beings who are stuck on destruction.

It is also a good idea to look at where you and your family are in resistance to letting go of energy and why. Another great thing to look at in meditation is where your family grounds through you – where is their control energy in your space and what are the underlying agreements? Then you want to end the karma and agreements so that you can have your own space and freedom.

GROUNDING THROUGH PICTURES, LEADERS, ORGANIZATIONS, AND HABITS

It is possible that your grounding cord tool is actually influenced, or set, by self-identity pictures you may have. Debra Lynne Katz explains, "When I was in the Philippines studying healing with the faith healers, that was my purpose, when I was in film school that was my soul purpose, when I published my first book, I had found my soul purpose as a writer. In all of these moments, I clung to this *concept,* this *notion, this picture* that I was doing my soul purpose because these thought forms made me feel safe. Essentially I grounded through these pictures."

It is also possible to ground through leaders and organizations; for example, it is very common when a leader of an organization leaves for many of the students or followers to leave as well. Those people were essentially grounding their participation in the organization *through* the leader. Usually if you are grounding through an organization there will be an underlying agreement as to why you are doing that.

My friend decided to tell everyone in her company that she wasn't going to be their "mom" anymore and the people that wanted to ground through her got upset and quit. If you own a business and all of your employees ground their jobs through you then your whole company can fall apart overnight if you have an accident. Once that grounding cord is no longer there they will feel that it is not safe to be part of the company any longer. Ideally, you want your employees to ground their commitment to their jobs through something else other than yourself. You can also be grounding through organizations you are no longer a part of anymore as well. Pictures, or ideas, like "I hope you will accept me back and let me into the group again in the future" can create agreements and situations where you are still connected to, and grounding through, an organization. Another example might be of a church official having an affair and lots of people leaving the church afterward. When something like that happens people will unconsciously get riled up about their own parents' divorces, and relationship issues, and staying neutral will be difficult, so they will take sides and leave the organization. Many followers are essentially grounding their spiritual commitments through their minister or leaders.

And some organizations may actually have leaders who are grounding through their followers. Some very prominent spiritual celebrities are doing this.

People who don't have grounding cords also tend to ground through habits, especially habitual movement patterns. If you don't consciously know how to ground then running all your habits will pull you into your body and into the predictable series of states of mind that you are used to;

essentially this is a way of returning to your habitual sense-of-self via your unconscious programming. When you know how to use a grounding cord then grounding through habits is no longer necessary.

Meditation Exercise: It's a good idea to clairvoyantly look at what self-identity pictures you ground through (if any) as well as any organizations, leaders, and habits you are grounding through.

MOVING OUT BLOCKS

Some spirits and even people may try to actually block, or control, your ability to ground yourself. So it is important to move them out of your energy body as well as get regular clairvoyant energy checks. If you are really stuck and it doesn't seem like you're releasing the energy in your space – it's just lighting up or getting more intense or you just feel it there constantly, but nothing else is happening, then you can create/imagine a rose and put any energy in it that says you can't ground. Then see it exploding. You may have to do this repeatedly for a while to move out that energy that is trying to block you. It really helps to have a couple other people help you out, give you feedback, and do clairvoyant healings – especially if you are working some really foul situation or intense energy.

Disasters and events that make people feel unsafe to be on earth can also affect grounding negatively. If you don't believe it is safe to be on this planet, or even in your neighborhood, then your grounding cord could get cut, stop working, or have some nasty beings snuggle into it. Ironically, this is the one time when grounding will help you the most. Getting out of fear and returning to a space of amusement and neutrality will help tremendously.

GROUNDING MORE OF THE VISIBLE LIGHT SPECTRUM

You may only be grounding the energy that you can see. Create a grounding cord and visualization in your next meditation to ground more of the light spectrum. I would advise doing this after you have some experience grounding.

ADDING TWICE AS MUCH GRAVITY

Postulate or imagine that your grounding cord is attracting and adding twice as much gravity to itself. This is an idea and a visualization that works well for some people and validates their grounding meditations. One person, however, told me that this did not work well for her and that it was too intense and messed up the balance and flow of her energy. Play around with it and see how it feels to you.

Chapter 6 – Next Steps

AVOIDANCE FEEDBACK LOOPS

It is possible for some people to move their awareness out of their bodies and simply stay in a pleasurable, empty, expanded state of mind. Empaths can usually do this easily. The problem is that foreign energy in your body tends to create pain. To release this you need to ground. However, if you have tons of pain in your body and your normal, or habitual, response is to move your energy and awareness even further away from your body then you create a kind of catch 22 situation – or feedback loop; the end result is that the more pain you're in the more you go out of your body – and consequently, the less you end up wanting to be present in your body. Coming down into your body, and making a strong commitment to do so, is the first step.

It took me a few years to actually make the commitment to do this because of all the depressing and reluctant emotions that were sitting in my body waiting for me – most of which weren't even mine. Coming into your body may be difficult if it is full of pain, energies, and images that you have to work through. Once you start making progress in releasing those unpleasant, stuck energies, you will start feeling lighter and better!

NOT GETTING ANYWHERE?

Do you ground for days and days and still feel like you are having trouble getting rid of a particular energy from your space? I would suggest getting a clairvoyant reading on it. I would also suggest changing your environment. This happened to me and it turned out that my feet chakras were just sucking in energy from my computer, which was right by my feet. Tons and tons of cold, fear-like energy and "data" energy would get sucked into my body through my feet. So all the hours and hours of grounding I did was more or less useless since I was just filling myself right back up with energy from my computer. I did not realize this was the case until I went on a month long vacation with no computers. I came back from vacation and sat down at the computer and then realized what was going on. There may be people or objects in your environment that act in the same way as my computer did. You may need to move out of your apartment, or your family or roommate situation, so that you are not in constant environmental exposure to the energy, or people, you want to move out of your space.

You may also have subconscious attachments, sub-personalities, investments, beliefs, or conflicts preventing you from releasing certain energies.

RUN EARTH AND COSMIC ENERGY

Grounding releases foreign and stuck energy from your space, but knowing how to bring in earth and cosmic energies is the next step. It will really help clear out your inner space. In fact grounding is really just the *first step in running earth and cosmic energy.*

DREAMS & GROUNDING

Before you go to sleep, pull up a bunch of earth energy into your whole body, through your feet chakras; let it permeate and fill your entire body. Your dreams will be very conscious and at times indistinguishable from reality. The trick to this is to be able to open your feet chakras and clean them out; they have to be opened enough to pull up a lot of earth energy. The downside is that your lucid dreams will be very straightforward and less "bright," because they will feel so close to reality; however, the advantage is that it can help you work on things in your dreams in a more concrete fashion.

YOUR NEXT STEP

Grounding is just one of many meditation tools, but it is the foundation upon which energy work lies.

If you can find a local community of clairvoyants I would highly recommend working with them. Or you can create your own community! The truth is that reading books about meditation can only give you a certain percentage of information and experience. Actually owning *all of the information in your body* requires practice; and working with professional clairvoyants in a safe space is an excellent way to own the information in this book.

My vision is for many people who have never heard of the concept of grounding to be able to have and use a grounding cord so that they can heal themselves and release what does not serve them. I have met many people who struggled to give to themselves, because they were giving so much to everyone else, and who desperately needed a grounding cord. I have met many people who were very spacey and benefitted tremendously from using a grounding cord. I know that my own life would have been so much easier had I known about this concept when I was a teenager struggling through high school.

So I hope you will share in this vision and share this book with your friends, family, and anyone who you think might benefit from grounding.

And if you're ready for more information I offer classes online to learn more advanced meditation tools and clairvoyant skills. Thanks for reading. I hope this book has validated you and your ability to ground and brought some new ideas to mind.

Visit my websites for more:

thrivemeditation.com

psychicclasses.org

thegroundingbook.com